ONCE UPON A TO Z

AN ALPHABET ODYSSEY

By Jody Linscott

Illustrated by Claudia Porges Holland

DOUBLEDAY

NEW YORK LONDON TORONTO SYDNEY AUCKLAND

Our most special thanks to Jacqueline Onassis and Shaye Areheart for making it really happen and helping so much!

Jody Linscott lives in London, England, where she works as a professional percussionist in the rock and roll industry. This book was inspired by her two little girls.

Claudia Porges Holland, a true New Yorker, is an artist, wife, and mother who divides her time between Manhattan and the Caribbean Islands, where she gets her color inspirations.

The illustrations in this book are all collages made with layers of colored paper.

DESIGNED BY PETER R. KRUZAN

PUBLISHED BY DOUBLEDAY a division of Bantam Doubleday Dell Publishing Group, Inc. 666 Fifth Avenue, New York, New York 10103 DOUBLEDAY and the portrayal of an anchor with a dolphin are trademarks of Doubleday, a division of Bantam Doubleday Dell Publishing Group, Inc.

Library of Congress Cataloging-in-Publication Data Linscott, Jody. Once upon A to Z : an alphabet odyssey / text by Jody Linscott; illustrations by Claudia Porges Holland. p. cm. Summary: In an alliterative text, the amazing appetite of Andy leads him to meet Daisy the delivery girl, with whom he forms the wonderful musical group, the Worthy Wonders. 1. Musical groups—Fiction. 2. Alphabet. I. Holland, Claudia Porges, ill. II. Title. PZ7.L663150n 1991 E—dc20 90-23495 CIP AC ISBN 0-385-41893-0 ISBN 0-385-41907-4 (lib bdg.) Text copyright © 1991 by Jody Linscott Illustrations copyright © 1991 by Claudia Porges Holland ALL RIGHTS RESERVED PRINTED IN THE UNITED STATES OF AMERICA OCTOBER 1991 FIRST EDITION

We dedicate this book to each other . . .
our fantastically faithful families
our kindhearted, kissable kids—
Coco, Kitt, and Kachina
and smiling Scott!

Andy always ate an astounding amount. Arti-chokes, apples, avocados and apricots, he ate anything at all, all afternoon. After a while his amazing appetite . . .

. . . became bigger and bigger and bigger and BIGGER!! His belly bulged and he bounced like a beach ball. He brought bags of bananas and biscuits to bed, burping between bites. Bit by bit, his bewildering behavior became unbelievable! By breakfast time it was . . .

. . . chaos! Clanking and crashing, he cooked clams, casseroles, crunchy corn on the cob and countless coconut-covered cupcakes! He certainly could create crazy concoctions, couldn't he?

Carefully clutching cocoa in a china cup, he chomped and chewed, content as a cow.

Of course, Andy . . .

. . . depended on dearest Daisy the delivery girl to dispatch dozens of delicious delicacies daily. One day, Daisy diddle-daddled and daydreamed from dawn till dusk and didn't deliver the delicacies. Dear oh dear.

By . . .

. . . evening at exactly eleven to eight the end-less edibles Andy enjoyed eating ended. He'd eaten everything entirely!

Exhausted and empty, he was . . .

. . . finally forced to face the facts—THE FOOD'S FINISHED—FIND DAISY FAST! Fumbling for his fuzzy frock coat, Andy fetched his favorite flashlight and fled to find his fickle friend through field and forest. He was . . .

. . . getting good and grouchy, but guided by great guessing he got going. Glancing at the ground he got goosebumps and gulped, "What's that gooey glob? Goblins? G-g-ghosts??"

Gaping at the glob, he giggled, "Good grief, gumdrops!"

Without a guess how the gumdrops got there, he gratefully gobbled them up.

"Hhhmmmm, hardly the hamburger I'd hoped for," he hiccuped. However, he hurried on happily until he heard a hair-raising HONK!! Had he heard a hideous hyena or a haunting harmonica? HONK HONK HWANK.

Horrors! He got the heebie-jeebies and hysterically hollered, "Help, help, a horrible honk! Help, help, a huge horrible hippopotamus is honking at me!! Help!!"

In his imagination, he'd invented an incredibly ill-tempered intruder! Instead it was Daisy innocently improvising on her impressive instrument. Andy interrupted her irately.

"Imp!" he said indignantly. "It's no . . .

. . . joke, jamming jazz in this jungle. I jumped with the jitters. And you just jeopardized your job by jilting me," jabbered Andy.

"Jeepers," said Daisy, jovially. "Join me for Jell-O and a jug of juice in my . . .

. . . kitchenette." She knew the kooky kitchen goods she kept in her kit were the key to keeping Andy okay, because she kept ketchup, kumquats, kidney beans, kitchenware, knockwurst, kettles, kindling, and a kerosene . . .

. . . lantern! A little later she lit the lamp. At long last after lengthy labor, Daisy laughed, "Look, luscious lasagna."

Andy loved lasagna and, no longer livid, he lunged longingly, lapping up a large load. Later, licking their lips, they lay low in a little lodging until . . .

. . . morning.

"Mmmmm," Andy mumbled, and moseyed over to mooch munchies.

"Morning, Mighty Mouth," murmured Daisy. "Munching more? Might I mention, moderation and manners may matter more than millions of measly meals?"

Nervously, Andy nodded.

"Naturally, there's no noticeable need for noodle-noggins," she nattered on. "Now, you need a new niche. Newspapermen are necessary. Nurses are noble. Nibblers are *not.*"

Andy nonchalantly named a number of nutty, . . .

. . . often outlandish occupations. Opportunities like outer-space orbiter, optician, or orthodontist often occurred to him. Optimistic and open for options, Andy . . .

. . . paused to ponder which particular project to pursue.

"Apart from peach pies and picnics, I prefer the piano," said Andy politely.

"Perfect," Daisy piped. "I play percussion!"

Pleased as punch, the pair plotted plans to perform publicly.

"Partners?" asked Daisy.

"Partners," promised Andy.

Quibbling quietly, they questioned the act.

"Quality or quits," Daisy quacked. "That's quintessential."

"Quite. 'Quality or quits,' " Andy quoted quickly. Then quaintly he queried the quantity of . . .

. . . refreshments they had reserved.

"I'm ravenous!"

"Remarkable," retorted Daisy, reaching for the remaining raisins. "You realize a respectable road show rehearses relentlessly, rarely resting. It's a rough routine. Are you really ready?"

Andy was rattled. "I'd rather . . .

. . . sing songs than sneak snacks," said he, solemnly studying a saucer full of sultanas.

"Speaking of songs," said Daisy, "since I squawk and squeak like a seasick soprano, suppose for the sake of the song we start searching for a sensational singer?"

Smiling simultaneously, they swiftly scampered off to sample some suitable singers for the show.

The twosome traveled to town to talk to the townsfolk about talented tenors.

"There are two to try," three talkative tattlers told them.

They telephoned the two to try out Tuesday.

At ten, in tumbled a two-ton toughie with two teeth and a terrible trill. Tactfully they told him no thanks. Then at twelve, tall Tilly tried the tune and thrilled them to tears with her tremendous technique, and today they're a trio!

This . . .

. . . unique unit was utterly underrehearsed until Daisy's Uncle Ulysses urged them to use his unusual utility room.

"Uncle Ulysses has an upright piano, a ukulele, and umpteen useful uniforms upstairs!"

"How 'bout umpteen upside-down cakes?" uttered Andy urgently.

Unanimously, they . . .

. . . voted to view it. They ventured in and, while Tilly vocalized with her versatile voice, Andy vanished! Vexed with visions of vegetables, he visited various vittle vendors. The vicinity was virtually vacant, but for a van vending vegetable juice. Revitalized, he vamoosed, then with vim, verve, and vigor, the vibrant virtuosos visited various village venues to volunteer their vibrant variety act.

They . . .

. . . wangled a whopping week's work that winter with wonderful wages as "The Worthy Wonders." When the Worthy Wonders worked they were welcomed with wild whistles! Well, Andy's waistline was waning and he wanted to waffle down whatever there was, so while working, the wacky weirdo wolfed down Daisy's wooden whatchamacallit!! The Worthy Wonders watched woefully as Andy winced. He wasn't well.

Whimpering, he wobbled to get . . .

. . . X-rayed!

The examiners exclaimed, "A xylophone!! It's a xylophone @#!*"

They Xeroxed the X-ray on Xmas day and the experts . . .

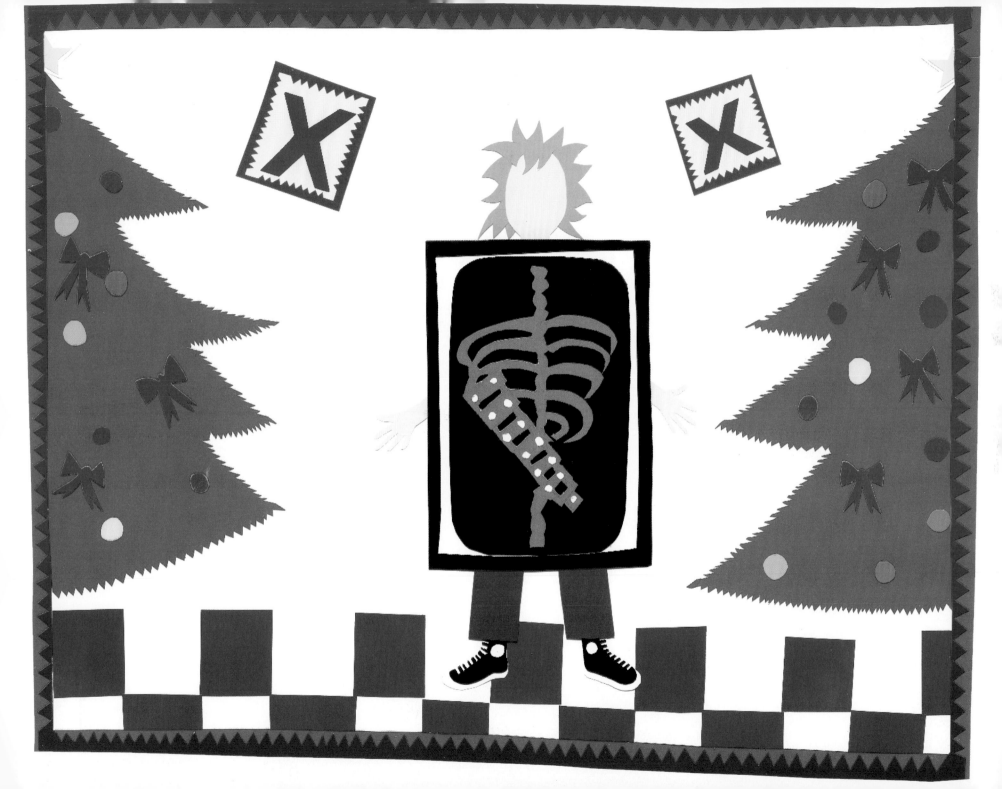

. . . yakety-yakked, yelping, "Yes! You'll be yellow as a yam this yuletide."

"Young man, you mustn't yield to your yearnings or you'll be yellow all year!"

"Yoiks," Andy yodeled. "All year?"

Yellow-bellied, he yowled, "Yesterday I yielded to yummy yearnings, but now . . .

Zero! Ziltch!"

Zestfully zippering his zebra-striped zoot suit, he zealously zipped back, and the zany trio zoomed to their zenith.

Andy, zonked and zapped out, zigzagged to bed and caught zillions of zzzzzzzzzzzzzzzzzzzzz-zzs . . .

. . . (with a zucchini pie of course).

GLOSSARY

Artichoke—A green vegetable
Astounding—Extremely surprising

Bewildering—Confusing
Bulged—Swelled out

Chaos—Utter disorder
China—Fine pottery
Concoction—Something made up
Content—Satisfied, happy
Countless—Too many to count
Create—To make

Delicacy—Tasty food
Dispatch—Send

Edible—Thing to eat

Fetched—Went to get
Fled—Ran away
Frock coat—Man's dress overcoat

Gaping—Staring
Glancing—Looking quickly

Hair-raising—Frightening
Heebie-jeebies—Fit of nervousness
Hideous—Very ugly
Hyena—A doglike wild animal

Ill-tempered—Cross
Imp—Mischievous child
Impressive—Awesome, remarkable
Improvising—Making up as one goes along
Indignantly—With righteous anger
Intruder—One who enters without permission
Irately—Angrily

Jabbered—Spoke rapidly
Jamming—Improvising jazz music
Jazz—Rhythmic popular music
Jeopardize—Endanger
Jilting—Discarding a close friend

Kerosene—A liquid that burns
Kindling—Lighting a fire
Kumquat—Small orange fruit

Measly—Small, scanty
Moderation—Not extreme
Mooch—Get without paying
Moseyed—Strolled along

Nattered—Chattered idly
Niche—Special place
Nonchalantly—Casually

Optimistic—Hopeful
Outlandish—Very strange

Pursue—Chase after

Quaintly—In an old-fashioned way
Queried—Asked
Quibbling—Raising small objections

Ravenous—Very hungry
Relentlessly—Continuously

Soprano—High singing voice
Sultana—Kind of raisin

Tactfully—In a considerate way
Technique—Way of doing
Tenor—Medium singing voice

Unanimously—All agreed

Vamoosed—Left quickly
Ventured—Dared
Venue—Place of a show
Versatile—Skilled in various ways
Verve—Enthusiasm
Vexed—Annoyed
Vibrant—Full of energy
Vigor—Force

Vim—Energy
Virtuoso—Very skilled
Vittle vendor—Food seller

Waning—Getting smaller
Whimpering—Crying softly
Woefully—Sadly

Xeroxed—Used a Xerox copying machine
X-ray—Picture of a person's insides

Yam—Root vegetable
Yellow-bellied—Cowardly
Yield—Give up
Yuletide—Christmastime

Zenith—Highest point
Zoot suit—Stylish men's wear